PRAISE FOR
THE VISUAL COMMUNICATIONS BOOK

'Mark is a visual dynamo – bringing alive often quite complex messages and simplifying into digestible chunks for the audience to understand and more importantly remember. His unique style and straightforward approach are a delight to experience and once encountered will never be forgotten.'

Jan Collins, Head of Business Network Services, Virgin Media

'Mark has worked closely with a variety of our sales teams with his approach to visual selling & communications. Having adopted his whiteboard approach our sales results have increased dramatically & I would highly recommend this book.'

Adam Sheppard, Managing Director, Toshiba TEC

'I first used Mark to help train one of my sales teams over 10 years ago. His style, even then, was littered with highly visual references which dramatically brought the training messages to life and, most importantly, made those messages 'stick'. His people development style & approach epitomises that 'every picture tells a thousand words'.'

Edward Kenny, Client Director, Computacenter

'We have successfully incorporated the advice given in *The Visual Communications Book*. It really can make all the difference in helping you to present complex ideas simply and easily.'

Mark Shephard, Director, Symantec Corporation

'Just one of Mark's visual strategies
helped me build a multi-million pound company
- imagine what a whole book of them
could do for your business'

Spencer Gallagher, Founder Cact.us, The Agency Growth Hackers

'The fastest and most effective way to explain something
is by drawing it. Mark is the undisputed champion
of explaining how to do this.'

Kevin Duncan, author, *The Diagrams Book* and *The Ideas Book*.

'I use my whiteboard sessions nearly every day in front
of clients. It helps them understand the USP of Vapour Media.
Incredibly powerful.'

Tim Mercer, Founder, Vapour Media

'In a world where we are overloaded with information
and face ever increasing competition for time and
attention, messages are routinely missed or
misunderstood. Mark's innovative and succinct approach
to visual communications cuts through the noise,
connects and works.'

Bill Shulby, Vice President, Global Learning

'This innovative approach to the art of visual
communication helps my teams deliver high impact
and innovative messages to their customers with
consistently excellent results.
You should read this book.'

Paul Fish, Director of Sales Enablement EMEA, Salesforce.com

'When Mark first approached me with some of his visual communications techniques I was a sceptic, but having seen them in action I quickly became a convert. I have now used them for more than 5 years in practice. I would strongly recommend these techniques to anyone wanting to deliver persuasive presentations...'

Chris Ducker, Head of Propositions Marketing, Europe, SunGard, Availability Services

To Wendy, Adam, Katie and Alice.

Thank you for all of your encouragement
and support over the years.

THE
VISUAL
COMMUNICATIONS
BOOK

USING WORDS, DRAWINGS AND
WHITEBOARDS TO SELL BIG IDEAS

MARK EDWARDS

LONDON MONTERREY
MADRID SHANGHAI
MEXICO CITY BOGOTA
NEW YORK BUENOS AIRES
BARCELONA SAN FRANCISCO

Published by
LID Publishing Ltd
Garden Studios
71-75 Shelton Street
Covent Garden
London WC2H 9JQ
info@lidpublishing.com
www.lidpublishing.com

A member of:

BPR
Business Publishers Roundtable

www.businesspublishersroundtable.com

Printed in the Czech Republic by Finidr

ISBN: 978-1-907794-94-0

Cover design: Laura Hawkins
Illustrations: Mark Edwards

CONTENTS

PART 4: VITAL CONCEPTS

FOREWORD

I was over 300 feet in the air when I first met Mark.

Seriously.

I was giving a talk on the 33rd floor of Centre Point in London, and he collared me afterwards.

The talk was all about how to win pitches with diagrams.

Mark said: *"I'm a great fan of pictures. I use them a lot myself."*

Or something pretty similar.

We got chatting, and it transpired that he was being somewhat self-effacing.

In truth, the man is an expert in visual communication.

He asked if I could advise him on how to publish a book on the subject.

I said I could.

And here it is.

It is based on a fundamental truth, and has important implications for any modern business.

If you really want to persuade someone, draw an engaging picture.

If you want to simplify a highly technical product, turn it into a visual.

If you want a whole salesforce to understand what you are
doing - you've guessed it - draw it.

Mark explains this extraordinary discipline in a way that ordinary people
like you and me can understand.

You don't have to be a world class artist to be able to do it.

You don't even have to be an amateur.

Just follow the steps he proposes and you could revolutionize
the way you approach presenting almost any case.

Let's cut the waffle and get drawing.

Kevin Duncan, author, *The Diagrams Book*

INTRODUCTION

From mankind's first cave drawings 40,000 years ago to the icons and signage you will find at any international airport in the 21st century, the world has always been full of man-made visual communications. Visual communications – for visual communicators and thinkers. That's you and me...

This book has been designed to act as a guidebook of sorts for people (again, like you and me) who prefer to present their ideas with visual imagery, shapes and graphics (as well as with words and numbers). It is clear that the most effective way to ensure that our ideas are understood by others is to use a visual aid to support our verbal or written explanations. As they say... a picture paints a thousand words.

For those of us who have not received formal training in graphic design it seems that our perspective regarding the presentation of ideas in business has been shaped by the ubiquitous PowerPoint – and its partner in crime, the Presentation Wizard: a dearth of words (arranged as hierarchical bullet points) and images (to be found in the 'where are they now?' clip art bargain bin) aggregated together, usually onto a vast number of slides.

My own personal background is in sales, leadership and learning, and development – so much of my time has been spent presenting and selling ideas, strategies, concepts, plans and proposals. At some point about 15 years ago, I naturally transitioned across into using visual drawings, charts, lists, illustrations and models to help me convey my ideas – and to persuade others to see and accept my point of view.

This book is intended to help you to do the same. I hope to encourage you to bring the creativity back into the way you present your ideas, your point of view – and ultimately yourself.

The book is physically small and can be quickly read in whole or in part, it can be flicked through, picked up, put down, loaned out, borrowed, cherished, well-used or even left to sit on your desk and used as a coaster... ☺

Although it is not intended to be the book of visual communications (I will leave that to the likes of data visualization pioneer Edward Tufte and others who have much greater knowledge and expertise than myself) – it may well be used by a number of you who are perhaps developing your own 'visual' style, repertoire and toolset. For some it may well be used as a book of simple 'standards and rules' (as no other such books exist) – and, for most, I hope it will act as a guide to which you will refer when looking for ideas or perhaps when considering the various options available to you as you try to get your ideas across.

I have used a graphics tablet to allow me to hand draw the illustrations and examples within the book because that is the way that I prefer to work. You may choose to use a pen, a mouse, a marker or a pencil to put together your own ideas. Whatever you do, just remember, it's not about art – it's about your ideas. Those are what count.

Always remember that **the true value of visual communications lies in its ability to help you to show - and not just tell - your story.**

PART 1

CUSTOM
STRUCTURES

PRESENTING SYSTEMS

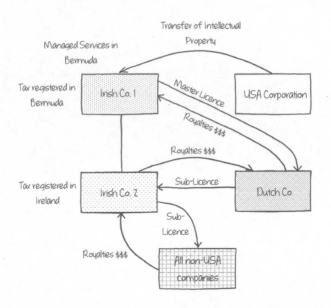

A system is a collection of individual parts or elements that are joined together in some way. The connections between the parts may be physical and objective (as in a diagram of an internal combustion engine or our solar system) or conceptual and subjective (as in a diagram of how peer pressure can influence the thinking, behaviour and actions of an individual). Or it may be a hybrid of the two (such as a diagram of a new computer network and how it will 'enable' workers and new capabilities) - part hard systems part soft systems.

Both systems thinking and systems engineering (with their visual and illustrative toolsets) have been developing rapidly since the 1980s and have been instrumental in the incredible advances in computing, finance, globalization, social policy, the internet, the World Wide Web and social media among other things.

Once individuals and teams are able to think in a systemic way, they are then able to communicate their thinking clearly to one another by using one of the more common visual communications tools such as pen and paper, whiteboards and computer applications like Visio, PowerPoint and others.

Presenting a system with an illustration or diagram can be incredibly powerful as it facilitates the clear communication of both simple systems and complex, abstract, conceptual systems.

So, how would you present a system?

Given that our ability to scale our drawings allows an individual to present something as large as our solar system on the back of a table napkin, it is important to consider your objectives. Are you looking to teach something? Persuade somebody of something? Engineer a group consensus and decision?

You will also need to identify the kernel of your message, as well as understanding the limits and boundaries of what you are presenting.

Consider your audience. What level of detail will they require? How knowledgeable are they? How much time will they have available?

Does the illustration of your chosen system need to be built with objective icons (like buildings, data centres, technical support staff and so on), or could you use various shapes, headings, arrows or connectors to construct the system? Could you use both and create a fusion of the two?

As you think about the system itself, use a pen and paper to sketch out and draw your ideas. You may well need to draw up a number of iterations of your system, stripping out superfluous information, grouping together smaller parts into their own sub-systems. Re-work it and re-work it until you think you've got it.

Aim to make it as simple and as elegant as possible. Be economical in your use of parts and texts. Ensure things don't look cramped by trying to squeeze in too much text; strip out stuff, or reduce the font size – or both.

Try to make your system 'easy on the eye' so that it piques the interest of your audience, as well as encouraging people to explore it further.

With a well-illustrated system you will find that you can massively reduce the amount of content and space required. While you may have previously created 15 slides to convey a message, you may now find that you can do better with two or three. All your thinking time will have paid off – and your audience will thank you.

Our example system here is an illustration of what is known as the Double Irish/Dutch Sandwich. It is a tax strategy that is employed by some of the largest companies in the world to help reduce the amount of tax payable in the Europe (with the UK being the biggest loser). In reality, the system is made up of corporate entities, licence agreements and bank accounts. There is no physical structure, just paperwork. The system diagram is the only way the system can be visualized in any way.

PRESENTING PROCESSES

A process is a series of actions directed towards a defined outcome.

As such, even making a cup of tea is a process. It entails a series of steps, some linear, some in parallel – all of which culminate in the creation of your favourite brew. Milk first or last? Alter the process. Fine china cup and saucer or mug? Alter the process further. Tea bag in the mug or loose leaf tea in the pot? You know the score...

Processes lend themselves to visual communication because the mapping out of processes is commonly achieved via process design tools and flow charts. Yes, a sequence of steps can be written down as in a cookery book, but more complex processes benefit from being presented as a flow chart. The flow chart method allows for multiple parallel processes, as well as accommodating multiple decision boxes and optional courses of actions. Thus, a flow chart is effectively a visual formula or algorithm which, in a programming context, means it can then be written out as computer code.

A visual presentation of a process is a very accurate form of communication, and in most instances it aids communication and ensures that all parties 'see' things the same way. By using standard symbols (like decision boxes and activity boxes) in the correct manner, a highly complex process can be mapped out and communicated to large groups – without loss of comprehension (as would often be the case in a set of complex written instructions).

So what are the benefits of presenting with a process or flow chart? Quite simply the key positives are understanding and appreciation.

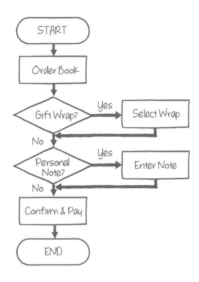

In many situations, complex processes are hidden away, and as a result, people often have little appreciation of the vast expenditure of energy that takes place to make something happen. That glass of orange juice you gulped down with breakfast this morning has probably travelled half way around the world to get to you. On the way, oranges have been squeezed, the juice pasteurized and packaged, shipped, distributed, stacked, bought and paid for – reliant on an infrastructure costing many billions of pounds.

Such complexity often escapes people, and there are many occasions when you (and they) will benefit from having a better understanding or appreciation of the steps involved.

Only 20 years ago, the idea of paying the price we do today for a large paper cup of milky coffee would have seemed absurd. The idea that most office workers would spend a sizeable sum each week on their coffees would have seemed illogical.

So how did Starbucks persuade people to do it?

Well, the brand was especially effective in educating customers about the nature of coffee production, the processes involved in harvesting, selecting, grinding, brewing and so on. While customers queued, waiting to be served, they were encouraged to handle the variety of coffee beans on show, and to look at the photos and their descriptions of the many processes involved in their production. Slowly, customers began to appreciate the value of such processes – and were primed to expect to pay more for this type of coffee. The description of the processes helped people to appreciate the value of the product.

Similarly, there are times when it will benefit your audience to understand the steps involved in a process, so that they fully appreciate the time something will take.

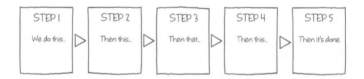

For instance, to get a new computer system installed by a certain date, it may be necessary for you to ensure that your customer understands the various steps and dependencies involved. If they choose to delay starting the process, they will surely understand that the completion of the project will be impacted.

Use of a process flow chart in this instance can be very effective in supporting your chosen perspective and point of view. If you make the case well enough, you can maintain a higher price point or get the decision you want taken immediately.

So how would you go about using visual processes as part of your communication?

Well, first consider what it is that you wish to present:
- Does the subject matter lend itself to a visual process flow chart?
- Will the communication objectives be better served by presenting the idea as a process?
- What elements of the process do you want people to understand better? Cost? Timescale? Necessary resources? Possible obstacles? The complexity of the process itself? Or, conversely, its simplicity? Something else?
- What are the alternative methods that could be used to present the matter?

PRESENTING INFOGRAPHICS

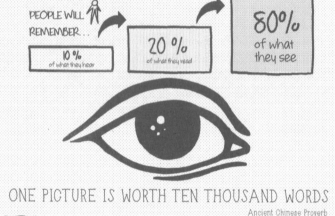

Infographics are highly visual representations of information. The data, information and points of view that are included are intended to provide the reader with a simple view of what may well be a very broad and complex subject (for example, worldwide population and nutrition statistics).

The infographic form lends itself to the effective representation of statistics and data, and is fast becoming the 'weapon of choice' for organizations (both commercial and political), media outlets (from magazines to newsrooms) and educators. British newspaper The Guardian often uses infographics to help readers understand complex issues such as economics, and TV news presenters are often found standing in front of giant screens waving at the infographic information behind them, beside them, and sometimes even beneath them (as part of some giant green screen CGI data-fest).

Infographics are most certainly 'in' as today's visual thinkers and communicators appreciate the look of an infographic and the speed at which large amounts of information can be scanned and taken in. Because of this in-built appreciation for the format, it is fair to say that today's readers of an infographic can be highly influenced by the information presented and by the perspective that the infographic originator wishes to promote. Because of the extensive and overt use of statistics, graphs and tables, an infographic has an air of academic or professional authenticity that is rarely questioned. Unless there is some clear dissonance between what the infographic claims and what the reader knows, the data is generally accepted as fact. However, there are many examples of infographics that intentionally misrepresent or skew data to push a chosen agenda or narrative. A quick look at the thousands of infographics that appear online will show that the facts presented are often no more than factoids (which, in my book, is a made-up statistic, just like when people quote the 80/20 rule about something for which they have no actual evidence). Some statistics look and feel too neat, too convenient.

As the legal expression "caveat emptor" recommends "buyer beware", today's infographics should come with a warning: "reader beware".

So, how could you use the infographic format to communicate your own ideas more clearly?

The basic premise involves breaking down a topic into a number of distinct areas, as an atlas would do when detailing population numbers, languages spoken, average attainment of education and so on, and then making a series of visually attractive points using a variety of tools such as numbers, statistics, words, graphs, maps, pie charts, bar charts, icons and more.

As you are likely to be using a computer to generate your infographic you will have more than 32 million different colours available to you – beware!

Key to making the infographic work is making it visually appealing – so choose a small, defined colour palette incorporating a number of complementary colours and tones.

To create an effective infographic use numbers, such as:

- Total numbers of things (For example, there are more than 30,000,000...)
- Percentages (56% of....)
- Fractions (three-quarters of...)
- Measurements (weight, volume, distance and so on)
- Multiples (three times as many...)
- Comparisons (one of these equals 42 of that)

These numbers must then be leveraged by using colour, font size, placement and comparison.

Link the number or statistic you have chosen to present with a suitable icon or image. The colour you choose here can also be used to help support your point (if it's a green issue, then it would make sense to use the colour green), as well as to form distinct information blocks. Each colour clearly denotes a single topic or category.

In terms of how to select data, and how to present it to best effect, the various types of visual tools and principles outlined in this book will be able to help.

Beyond the visual appeal of the infographic, its potential lies in the way in which data is presented. Positive or negative comparisons can be made. Relative size can be used to accentuate, or even stretch, a point. Emoticons, icons and images can be used to evoke suggested emotional states. The possibilities are endless.

The title you give your infographic is also very important in terms of framing your point of view. Make your point in the title, and then use other tools to support the point you wish to make. If, however, your aim is to be more subtle, then select a title that presents the infographic as being independent or undecided on the issue.

Infographics are incredibly useful for many reasons. They are best presented in a printed format (book, magazine, newspaper, poster and so on), online or as a slide projection.

Used carefully, an infographic can effectively frame a topic and set the context and narrative for future use.

PART 2

GENERIC
TOOLS

COMMON FRAMEWORKS AND STRUCTURES

There are many common frameworks and structures that can be used to form part of your visual communications.

Certain structures lend themselves to specific types of information. For instance a Boston Matrix/Four Quadrant framework is great when dealing with two axes of variable data points. You can quickly and easily slot your information into the structure and most people will generally understand how the information is to be read, without needing additional instruction. Those of us who have spent many years in business will have seen all the common frameworks presented here.

These structures can form the central plank of your presentation, or they can be used in a supporting role to define and articulate your point, support your claim or to bend the opinions of your audience.

Some of these frameworks come pre-loaded with a scientific or mathematical 'halo effect', and so you can use this to support your point of view. In the minds of many people: if it looks like maths, sounds like maths – then it must be maths.

Here are some of the most commonly used frameworks:

THE VENN DIAGRAM
This structure, which is introduced to most people when they are at school, is a useful tool for showing the similarities and differences between two or more sets of data. It is easy to understand and, due

to its use in education, it also confers some of the mathematical halo effect mentioned earlier.

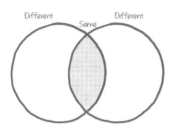
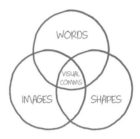

THE TRIANGLE
Take three topics, concepts, strengths, weaknesses (or whatever) and place one at each point of a triangle and, hey presto, you have created a powerful triad model. Be it 'knowledge, skills and attitude (KSA)', or the project manager's favourite of 'quality, time and cost' – this is a handy approach to bringing together three related, but different, items.

PYRAMID
There are various ways of using a horizontally tiered pyramid to support your point.

One approach is where the layers represent varying volumes. The lower levels would indicate the greater volumes, and the cap stone indicates the lowest volume.

Another approach is, again, to build from the bottom up, but this time using the layers to represent various levels of dependency or superiority as you travel up through the pyramid. In this approach, the layers do not indicate volume or quantity in any way.

Perhaps the best known pyramid model is Maslow's Hierarchy of Needs. Indeed, it is likely that this model would have disappeared without a trace had it not anchored itself to the pyramid structure. Maslow's simple act of integrating his theory with a pyramid structure meant his concept could be easily understood and communicated.

MIND MAP
Tony Buzan popularized the mind map or spider diagram in the 1980s and 1990s. It is now often used in schools as a method for brainstorming – and even for organizing ideas. Personally, I find it useful only for brainstorming as there are smarter ways to organize and structure information. The main issue for me is that the connections in a mind map diagram are, to my mind, suggestive of a loose and fluid association – although there are, of course, times when this may well be of use.

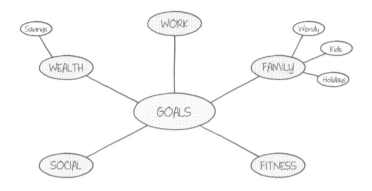

THE ONION
No, not the satirical online magazine, but the graphical framework.

The model is typically circular (so not exactly like an onion) and presents a group of concentric circles radiating out from a central core. The framework can be used to present a layering of themes, and can also represent various objects and subjects and their association to the central core (with the distance between items representing the depth or strength of connection and association).

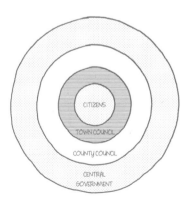

THE PIE CHART

A useful structure with many uses. In common usage, it tends to be sub-divided into three, four or more equal segments. It is easiest to view when presenting slices in blocks of thirds, quarters or halves. This way it can be used to present different topics or categories – albeit under the one umbrella.

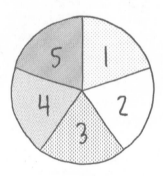

THE DOUGHNUT

The doughnut is the younger sibling of the pie chart. It works to the same principles, but with a neat hole removed from the centre (in which you can place the title or an icon).

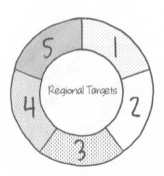

ORGANIZATION OR HIERARCHY CHART

An organization or hierarchy chart is commonly used to present the structure or reporting lines within an organization or enterprise. However, the structure has other uses, and can be used very effectively to show the hierarchical principles at play in other areas.

Fluency and understanding of the various frameworks and structures presented here is a real boon – and it is well worth playing with these models and seeing exactly how far you can push them.

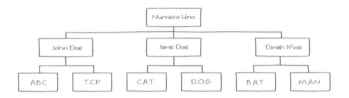

GRAPHS

Line graphs are useful tools for visual communications. Graphs themselves are formed from a collection of ordered pairs of coordinates, along two axes (x and y). A graph can be created to present information in a way that is truly informative (leaving the viewer to draw their conclusions), or to present information in a way which is less open to interpretation, and instead is intended to be supportive of a chosen viewpoint (in this case, the graph is typically used to support a claim, a conclusion or to underpin the case being made by the author).

Once plotted on the graph itself, the coordinate points can be connected by lines to illustrate visually the data being presented; this is typically how mathematical model graphs are presented. Like me, you may have memories of graph plotting and drawing from your school days. Oh joy of joys...

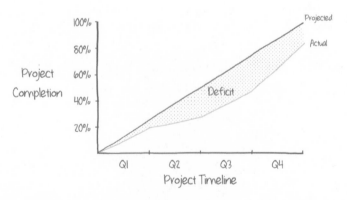

As part of our science culture, it is also expected that all data points used should be factual and correct. Because of this, a graph-based model suggests solid data, mathematical integrity and the highest level of attention to detail. A graph infers data integrity and confers this integrity to the graph producer. This is the point at which science and art intersect; but, perhaps, where science and spin can also intersect.

There have been a number of disparaging quotes about statistics and their use over the years, but there do not seem to be any about the use of graphs. However, a graph has even greater persuasive potential than a simple statistic.

The basic graph model of two axes can be used in a variety of ways to present various forms of collected data. The graph line is commonly used to represent the trajectory of a set of collected data (volume of sales, x-axis; the weeks in a month, y-axis) – which will typically be presented as a line moving from left to right. The data from previous years can also be plotted along the same axes in a different colour to provide context (perhaps to flatter today's figures, or maybe to justify them).

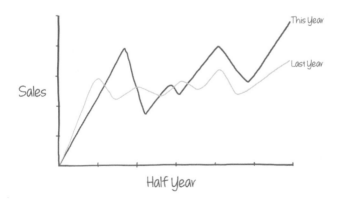

Another common form of graph is what is sometimes called the Boston Matrix. This is a chart that was created in the 1970s by the Boston

Consulting Group to help companies analyze their product lines and to enable them to make better decisions about their resource allocation. This type of graph is used to plot separate coordinates that represent separate units.

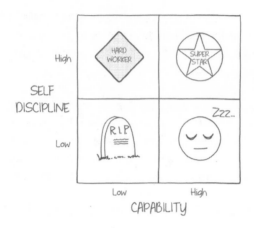

The quadrant or matrix layout lends itself to the creation of categories or labels for the various segments, or segments within segments.

The measurement systems regularly used in this type of matrix are often determined by the matrix creators, so there is less (possibly no) external scrutiny applied. Subjective criteria or characteristics can, in this way, be presented as scientific, statistical or even mathematical. It is often the case that the more academic and detailed the graph or model, the greater the credibility gained.

On the other hand, the use of the quadrant or matrix layout, with its easy presentation of categories or labels, can be a positive boon in aiding the presentation of abstract ideas or forms. It presents the information in a less academic or scientific way.

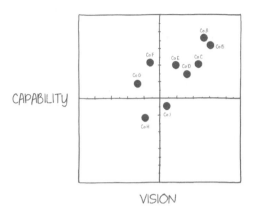

There are many, many uses for graphs – so a graph can often be seen as the kernel of an academic theory, as well as the capstone of many a business case. Opinions can be shifted or firmed-up, discussions impacted and directed - and important, mission-critical decisions made as a consequence of a graph.

Use them wisely.

VISUAL METAPHORS, ANALOGIES AND SIMILIES

A metaphor is generally understood to be a figure of speech. It is a way of describing something by relating it to something else. In doing so, it aims to show that a specific characteristic is common between the two. The common characteristic (or characteristics) can be simple or complex, clear to see or somewhat opaque. It can relate to a similarity of a physical nature, its use and application, its make-up, its constituent parts, its history – or indeed its future. To say that "law and its application is the foundation stone upon which civil society is built" is to use a metaphor – with the comparison to foundation stones being metaphorical. The traits being acquired are strength and solidity.

To see life as being a *journey* which requires clear *direction* is metaphorical in a number of ways. As with all things, the metaphor can be stretched too far very easily; all that is needed is to keep adding elements such as the need for *suitable travel companions or provisions* to complete the journey and you can see how overburdened the metaphor can become. This undermines its use as a rhetorical and conceptual tool.

A comparison can also be drawn using an analogy.

If a metaphor is used to compare characteristics, an analogy is used to compare more practical, mechanical and physical characteristics. To say that human societies can be compared to bee colonies in terms of the social structure (or vice versa) is to use an analogy.

In a number of ways, a bee colony is analogous to human society.

Third, we have similes. A simile is like a metaphor in that it compares a characteristic, but it uses a connecting word to make the comparison. If we say that "the challenges we face are like an iceberg where two thirds remain submerged from view" we are using a simile.

In visual communications, the use of a visual metaphor – or an analogy or simile – is especially powerful, as it effortlessly supports the point you are trying to make. In some instances, this type of device can be used to support a trait and encourage your audience to accept it – even though the similarity is inaccurate. This is not something I would recommend, but it is surely worth being aware of it. The next time someone refers to a "customer journey" try to apply some critical thinking to the metaphor, rather than simply accepting the suggestion.

Common visual metaphors, analogies and similes used in business presentations include:

The tightrope: this can be used in a number of ways:
- To promote the need for careful progress along a path
- To convey the potential dangers of failure
- To present the need for a safety-net.... just in case
- To highlight the need to keep the end goal in sight
  (and not look down)

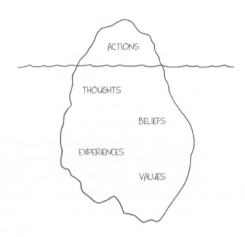

The iceberg:
- Much of the iceberg remains hidden from view
- The object of greatest significance lies below the water's surface
- Failure to appreciate the dangers of the 'iceberg' can prove costly (invoking the memory of the sinking of the Titanic)

The temple structure:
- A building or structure of any substance requires firm foundations
- Upright pillars are needed to keep the structure solid and to maintain a strong rooftop capable of repelling those nasty elements ;-)
- The better the materials used, the stronger the structure

The jigsaw puzzle:

- To complete the puzzle, all the constituent parts need to be locked into place
- Each piece has a specific place where it 'fits'
- No pieces should be forced into the wrong position – or perhaps this idea is better explained by referencing "putting a square peg into a round hole" – but then I am mixing metaphors....

The visual metaphor, analogy or simile can help provide a framework or structure for your point, subtly adding meaning and assurance to the concept or perspective you are trying to explain.

VISUAL MECHANISMS

A visual mechanism is a useful graphic device that can be used to present or imply that a change in data will produce a change in output or outcome. The most common visual mechanism is a see-saw; which might also be represented as a weighing scale. Typically, this specific device is intended to show how a state of equilibrium can be established or jeopardized; too much of 'this' means imbalance, and too little of 'that' means imbalance.

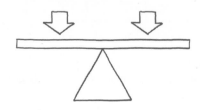

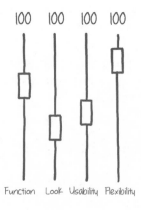

Similarly, a set of volume controllers (presented either as dials or sliders) can be used to indicate changeable inputs. A set of sliders can be set to show a set of specific levels or inputs – and then edited to show a different set of inputs. Discussions around the impact of the potential changes in inputs can take place alongside a single image – and the potential changes in inputs can be simulated by using hand movements and engaging your audience's imagination to visualize the suggested change.

In its most basic form a visual mechanism can be used to represent a single, yardstick-like input: similar to the way that the speedometer in your car presents you with a dial with measures and a pointer to show you how fast you are travelling.

At the other end of the spectrum, we have the potential for more complicated, systems-like mechanisms whereby changes in inputs can be used to shift a balance which is then used to provide a read-out on yet another yardstick. Again, by building this type of mechanism into a discussion, the various inputs and potential effects can be simulated, implied, overlaid or just imagined.

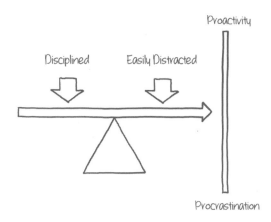

COUPLING MECHANISMS

A coupling mechanism is a device used to yoke or couple together two separate elements of a graphical illustration. There are a various ways in which this can be done – and a variety of uses too.

In some instances, the coupling effect takes place just by placing various elements close to one another (as in the diagram below where the inputs onto the see-saw present a form of read-out to which you can add by the positioning of one or even two additional vertical measures). In this way, a visual read-out is presented via the see-saw or balance – as well as on the vertical measure (or measures).

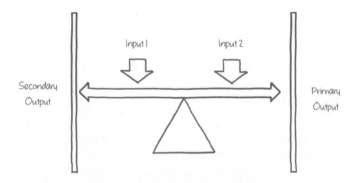

Another effective way of coupling is to insert a visual yoke into the illustration to create a more physical coupling effect – much as a tow-bar joins a car to a trailer. In the example opposite, the coupling device is used in the form of a triangle. Its insertion into the two-part diagram adds a third element which effectively hitches itself to the circle – and hey presto, it forms a movable dial that can be considered to move either left or right, highlighting various points on the horizontal measure that sits above it.

Used as part of a presentation to an audience, the final coupling effect can create a powerful "Aha!" experience when the enlarged view or perspective is integrated and understood.

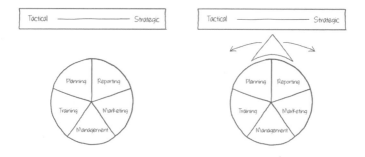

PART 3

PHYSICAL
CONSIDERATIONS

COLOURS

Colour has many applications in the world of visual communications. From signifying certain traits, to making things more aesthetically pleasing, colour, when used correctly, can have a powerful impact.

When working with a full palette of colours (such as you would have at your disposal when using PowerPoint or any other presentation application) you have many options available to you. Certain colours have certain associations. Green in many situations would signify a positive – a green 'go' light for instance. Similarly, red can be seen as signifying heat or something dangerous or restrictive (as in a red 'stop' light).

Common associations for each colour include:
- **Red:** Passion, strength, excitement, "stop!", "pay attention!"
- **Orange:** Warmth, friendliness, spirituality, balance
- **Yellow:** Happiness, fun, cheer
- **Green:** Nature, environment, calm, "go!", envy
  (as in "green with envy")
- **Blue:** Stability, royalty, authority, coldness
- **Purple:** Romanticism, mysticism, nobility, royalty
- **Brown:** Earthiness, warmth, nature, rusticity
- **Black:** Sophistication, power, modernity, darkness, evil
- **White:** Purity, innocence, truth, peace

A thoughtful use of colour will also ensure certain elements of your design stand out, by dint of being a different or contrasting colour to those surrounding them. You can also use a variation in colour to draw attention to certain words, phrases and so on.

In a more limited world (for example, when using a whiteboard or flip chart) you might have to make your selection from a smaller palette of four colours (red, blue, green and black) or even fewer when writing a book in simple black and white.

The various colours can be used to highlight and to convey certain meaning, but colour can also be used to establish and present categories. When presenting three short bullet point lists, using a different colour for each list suggests difference for all others – but it also suggests a similarity or affinity with similarly coloured points.

Where you are restricted to one or two colours (as in the production of this book) you can use shading, stripes or spots to create differentiation. You can increase the number of shades you have at your disposal – although the ability to convey associations (as you can by using colours) is lost.

• LIGHTS	• EGGS	• STRINGS
• PLUGS	• JUICE	• CASE
• BULBS	• COFFEE	• LEADS
• FUSES	• MILK	• PEDALS

CONTAINERS

A word that is shown as part of a group of words on a plain, contrasting background has just its font style, size and colour to help it make its impact on the viewer. Enlarging or reducing the font size has a noticeable effect, as does changing the font itself to one of the hundreds of thousands that exist today. The colour used and its contrast with the background can also change the way a word or image is perceived and understood. A light grey word presented against a plain white background has a very different impact to the same word presented in red and placed on a black background.

Another way of influencing how words and images are perceived by viewers is to present them inside a visual container. The choice of containers used, their shape, size, colour and relative position in your illustration, provides scope for creating additional impact and meaning. In this way, it is possible to highlight one word out of many and to evoke additional and peculiar characteristics. Is a word placed in a tight-fitting rectangle or in a medium-sized circle? A free-form, blob-like container as opposed to a quadrilateral shape comprised of straight-lines and hard angles? A triangle or a circle?

The shape, colour, line type and size of the container can all be varied to have an impact and affect meaning.

The Visual Communications Book

As part of one of my own presentations, the acronym 'VP' (meaning a 'value proposition') was written in block capitals using a black marker pen. At the same time as explaining to the audience that what we do "is to help codify and give shape to a proposition" I drew a red circle, purposely and precisely, around the two letters. The combination of the letters on the board, the commentary alluding to the verb 'to shape' – and the actual drawing of a shape (in this instance, a circle) all combined to deliver maximum impact and a clear understanding.

LINES AND ARROWS

Lines and arrows can do more than just connecting items and indicating direction; they have many uses for today's visual communicator.

Lines can also be used:

To connect two or more items. Consider the complexity and volume of information that is contained within a simple organization chart; names in boxes are linked via vertical and horizontal lines using a well understood hierarchical protocol. The simplest of lines, in the right situation, can help illuminate an abstract idea and bring it to life.

To separate and partition. If money really does make the world go around then it's safe to say that 'lines' make the money-go-round (did you see what I did there...?).

As an example of the power of a line, consider this: a single, vertical line on a page, dividing the page into two columns, creates a simple balance sheet (assets and liabilities) which is the basis of modern accounting methods worldwide. Just add a couple of horizontal lines in each column to separate items and create some sub-totals and you are nearly there. Now we just need the numbers, the cash, and an offshore holding company structure and we are on our way to our very own Double Irish/Dutch Sandwich.

Used in accordance with a well-known accounting protocol like this – just one line can create miracles.

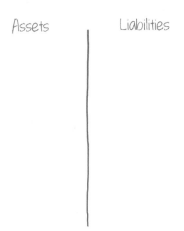

To underline and emphasize things. For instance, among a series of words, a line can be used to emphasize and focus attention. The same line can also be moved upwards slightly to strike through the word, representing a removal or rejection of an item.

To create tables, columns and rows. There is no limit to the various ways in which you can use and integrate tables, columns, rows and swim-lanes to help present information to your audience.

How to create real, lasting value...

Arrows can also be used:

To represent the direction of travel being taken. When used in a system or process illustration, arrows are necessary to indicate the directions taken by the various forces, flows or elements being presented.

As visual shorthand for adjectives. Meaningful icons can be created by placing an up or down arrow alongside something else. A dollar sign with a down arrow beside it can effectively be used to infer or claim a reduction in cost. Similarly a data storage icon (in the form of a drum) with an up arrow can be used to indicate data growth.

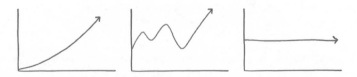

As part of a graph to present various states. The plotted graph line arrow can be used to present a variety of states. Wild fluctuations can be presented by extreme peaks and troughs; downward or upward trends can be easily presented by a simple curve, and exponential growth can be shown by use of a sharp, hockey-stick curve.

EMOTICONS

Since the introduction of text messaging, the world has been besieged by myriad emoticons. The emoticon is a textual way of presenting a visual representation of an emotion: happy, sad, bored, amused, and so on.

The 1960s and 1970s saw the introduction, and growing popularity, of the 'smiley' – a yellow, happy face which, for a time, became a form of pop art, a global cultural phenomenon. It has never left us, and is still frequently used today. In fact, it saw a resurgence in the early 1990s as it was associated with the new rave culture – the music and associated drug taking.

It is from this original smiley figure that today's happy, frowning and winking emoticons derive.

In terms of usage in modern day business communications and presentations emoticons or traditional smilies can be used to support a point of view, and even to persuade an audience to accept something as either being 'good or bad'. These symbols work in a similar way to a tick, a cross or a question mark which are used to suggest things are wholly good or right, wholly bad or wrong – or questionable.

The happy or frowning emoticons are simple to draw by hand and so their use as part of a hand drawn (or written) communication is especially effective. A smiley drawn alongside a number on a whiteboard is a clear instruction to accept the number as good or accurate. The reverse is also true.

Smilies are easy to draw – and their meaning is universally understood. Put them to work.

EXPRESSIVE SHAPES

The most common shapes used in visual communications are squares, rectangles, circles and triangles. Although, in some contexts, these shapes would add additional meaning to your communication, they tend to remain relatively neutral; they are just part of the portfolio of shapes that people might use or encounter.

However, there are other more expressive shapes that can be used to add meaning, to direct your audience's thinking (as well as its attention) – and to make the desired impression.

Cartoons and comics make great use of expressive shapes to illuminate their images and to bring them to life. A star here, a larger star there, a cloud burst here, a speech bubble with the word "BAM!" in it and so on.

Lightning bolts carry a lot of potential meaning when used in the right way. With the addition of some fiery colours this simple shape can be used to express power, energy and surprise.

A thought cloud beside a person, or a series of clouds floating away into the distance, can be used to express more ethereal meaning.

USING PHYSICAL GAPS

It has to be said that the use of physical gaps is one of my favourite tools in a visual presentation. The gap begs for closure. It infers lack or a failure of sorts. The bigger the gap, the bigger the problem. The bigger the problem, the bigger the likely solution.

Closing or reducing the gap infers that progress is being made or has been made. Where a gap is presented correctly, people automatically recognize a problem to be solved. This is not just for the analytically minded. It works as well with more emotional individuals. As an example, consider Al Gore's Oscar-winning documentary An Inconvenient Truth. The crux of the film's message hung on Gore's famous 'hockey stick' curve which showed a widening gap between current greenhouse gas emissions and projected future emissions. It then linked the projection to an apocalyptic vision of global warming, the thawing of the ice caps and the extinction of the polar bear. A graph was used to great effect to enlarge and extend the gap and to help promote Gore's point of view. He even wheeled in a cherry picker so that he could be lifted up alongside the graph to hammer home that size of the gap.

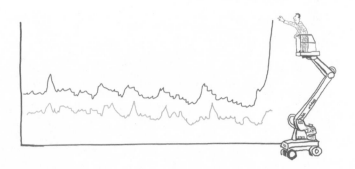

A gap is meant to represent a disparity of sorts. It can be a gap between the current, 'as is' situation and the future, desired 'to be' situation. This gap can be portrayed in physical terms even when the two states are conceptual and have no physical characteristics as such.

A gap can also be presented in numerical terms. The beauty of this method is that we can create our very own, specific terms of reference. For instance, I can ask someone, "On a scale from one to ten (with ten being expert and one being novice) how would you rate your financial management skills?" Let's imagine the response is a five.

This can then be followed up with a future-based question such as, "In a perfect world, where would you like your financial management skills to be in one year's time?" The answer would typically be a seven or an eight. Ok – now what do we have? Yes, you got it. A gap! And the closure of that gap is now the context for presentation.

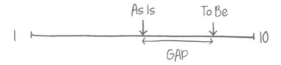

The numerical gap can also be given some physical characteristics by turning the numbers into a representative scale. A horizontal line can be drawn to represent the one-to-ten scale and then marks can be inserted to represent the numerical gap. The longer the length of the line used for your scale, the bigger the gap between the 'as is' and 'to be'. Even a gap of two points (for example, from five to seven) can be made to look wide when placed on a sufficiently large scale. Presented vertically, you might even need to wheel in a cherry picker to help you present this enormous gap... ;-)

This is a powerful tool when used effectively. Used inappropriately, it can be damaging to your cause. Begin by identifying a number of areas in which the use of physical gaps might work and start to play with them. Most importantly, put them to use with other people. Use them in conversation, in presentations, on flip charts and on whiteboards when in meetings. Mastering 'the gap' is likely to bring you great success. Use it responsibly.

ANTHROPOMORPHISMS

The very earliest cave drawings related to human beings and their activities.

As children, growing up, we drew literally hundreds (or possibly even thousands) of people. The contents of the picture and the situations portrayed varied greatly, but the roles, circumstances and experiences of the human in the drawing was always central.

People relate to characters in books, adverts, in TV programmes and films; characters who are like us and also characters whom we admire and would like to be like. The connection is powerful, automatic and yet subtle.

By using the human form in visual communications, it is possible to tap into the natural empathy people have for other people (a third party) and, with a subtle shift of perspective, it is also possible to encourage people to put themselves into the picture and to participate emotionally in the situation as if it were them (in the first person).

Managed correctly, a kind of transference can take place, which leads to a very powerful form of experiential (albeit imaginary) communication.

Generic stick people are particularly effective for this type of situation as they have no distinguishing features, unless you want them to have these; for example, a walking stick to signify old age.

Feel free to play with this form as you create visual environments that are appropriate for the message and meaning you aim to communicate.

To communicate vision, place a stick man standing at the summit of a mountain pointing into the distance.

To communicate indecision, place your stick man at a fork in the road with a question mark above him.

A stick man walking along a tightrope has many meanings – but is mostly to signify the need for special care as a wrong step could be fatal.

To achieve the transference element, the visuals really need to be supported by a written or verbal narrative. This narrative gives people the cue or instruction about how to interact.

For instance, having drawn a stick man, the verbal or written instruction of, "Imagine this is your customer", will ensure the person receiving the message will fill in the mental gap by inserting a third party (a customer in this instance) into the image. Your audience is involved, but remains detached.

Your Customer

Similarly, having drawn a stick man at the left-hand side of a horizontal line (symbolizing time or maybe a process journey), the verbal or written instruction of: "This is you; you are at the beginning of a complex process with many potential obstacles ahead", will instruct your audience members to think in first person terms regarding the situation you are describing. They put themselves 'in' the picture.

Both of these have many uses when it comes to explaining, persuading or teaching others.

IMAGES, WORDS AND NAMES

There is a classic sales exercise called "the Benjamin Franklin" close. In this exchange with a potential customer, the sales person invokes the name of one of the founding fathers of the US, Benjamin Franklin, before taking the customer through a process whereby a list of the proposal's pros and cons is drawn up on a sheet of paper.

Part of this exercise's efficacy comes from the advantage (and cover) it gains from its association with, and its invocation of, Uncle Ben.

Benjamin Franklin

This is not dissimilar to how celebrities with particular credentials are used to promote certain products and services. The product manufacturer is attaching the celebrity's credentials, reputation and meaning to their product or service.

When creating your visual communication, there is sometimes an opportunity to use specific words, images or names to evoke certain characteristics in order to influence your audience.

An image of a doctor inspires trust and confidence. Quoting or representing certain people (or even types of people) can then be used to enhance your communication.

You will see this being used in a wide variety of situations. An image of, or even a written quote from, iconic figures such as Mahatma Ghandi, or Martin Luther King Jr can be used to lend moral authority to a presentation. Some people are synonymous with certain characteristics or outcomes. Modern examples include:

Sir Richard Branson, Lord Alan Sugar, Peter Jones – entrepreneurism
Steve Jobs – creativity and success
Bill Gates, Warren Buffet – wealth
Jessica Ennis-Hill – fitness and vitality
John Lennon – idealism
Thomas Edison – inventiveness
Albert Einstein – intelligence

Similarly, the words, images and names of Adolf Hitler, disgraced TV personality Jimmy Savile and convicted child-killer Myra Hindley evoke negative emotions and connotations.

In some instances, an image of the individual will be necessary. In others, just drawing a simple doodle or writing up their name on a whiteboard will suffice. The situation will determine which form will work best.

PART 4

VITAL
CONCEPTS

CONCEPTUAL CONSIDERATIONS

Regardless of your actual intention, your audience will infer meaning from the way in which you organize and present information. As a result, a well-considered approach is recommended, even if the meaning you wish to convey relates to improvisation. ;-)

To avoid unanticipated and incorrect associations you will need to plan the visual relationships in your graphical design, as well as the verbal relationships and connotations in your accompanying narrative or commentary.

People tend to fail to plan such things because it does not occur to them to do so. Hence, in this section of the book, we are going to look at the various elements that will affect the way your audience perceives your communication.

It is important to consider how to direct your audience's need to understand what they see and hear – and effectively use a playbook of 'conceptual considerations' to achieve your communication goals and objectives. These considerations include things like colour, size, proximity, symmetry, order and sequence.

By using the tools presented, you can support your communication and increase the likelihood of achieving your objective. By failing to use these tools consciously, you are increasing the likelihood of your audience coming to an arbitrary or erroneous conclusion. Just think how many propositions and proposals have failed in their final presentation. Was it because the idea or concept was ill-considered?

Sometimes, but not always. Many ideas fail because of the meaning your audience members take away from the presentation. They may not even be able to explain why they didn't like the idea or the presentation specifically. It might simply be that there was something in it that unsettled them, or they felt something undermined the presentation or presenter. This is similar to the feeling we might get when somebody tells us one thing – but we believe another. Somewhere, in the middle of the verbal and visual cues, there is something that we just know is not right, is not in keeping with the message, or in keeping with the presenter.

Yes or No?

THE OBSERVER'S SHARE

The well-known Zen koan, "If a tree falls in a forest and no one is around to hear it, does it make a sound?", is instructive in this instance. Or maybe the question relating to the 'sound of one hand clapping' works better? You decide...

Appropriate consideration needs to be given to your audience. What preconceptions, prejudices, agenda, beliefs and so on do members carry with them? Art students are often reminded to be conscious of the "observer's share" which relates to the way the audience will view and interpret their work. Any work on its own, in isolation, is devoid of meaning. It is only through the perception of a viewer that an image can come to life.

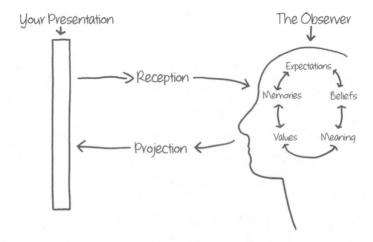

Certain symbols, shapes and words are loaded with meanings, positive and negative. Some meanings are cultural and understood by all in that culture; some are unique to the individual. Other meanings represent something different depending on context.

A cartoon sequence drawing of a pencil, followed by an image of a pencil snapped in two – and then the two halves being sharpened to become two pencils means something very different and emotive in the aftermath of the shootings, by Islamist terrorist group Al-Qaeda, of journalists at the offices of satirical magazine *Charlie Hebdo*, in Paris. Following such an event, the image of a lone pencil can evoke feelings and meaning.

SIZE

It's been said before... size matters!

Studies have shown that a man's height has an impact on his overall lifetime earnings. Whether this has to do with tall men having increased confidence, or with other people's perceptions and judgments about size, it appears that for each inch of additional height, the taller man will earn an extra $5,000 a year, on average, than his shorter colleague.

An observer brings a large bag full of their own prejudices, experiences, beliefs and values to every interaction. Size is one of those factors upon which people rarely reflect consciously, but which undoubtedly has a bearing on perception.

As a characteristic of a visual form, size can be presented literally, to represent real scale, or figuratively, to represent other characteristics (such as superiority, inferiority, importance, relativity to other elements and so on). The size of something may purely relate to the scale or look of the image, or it may be used to suggest meaning, to evoke an emotion, or to persuade or prove a point.

The size of objects cannot fail to affect a perceived relationship between the objects. This relativity is important and needs to be built into your overall communication objectives. Size can be used to bring focus and attention to specific characteristics and content – while it can also be used to obscure others.

So, how best to use size to help support your objective?

Ask yourself:

- Am I working with words, images or shapes?
- If size impacts people's perception of importance or hierarchy – which parts of my overall message would benefit from an increase in size?
- Alternately, what, if anything, would benefit from being reduced in size?

PROXIMITY AND DISTANCE

Typically, the less space there is between two items, then the stronger we perceive the relationship, connection or bond to be. In other words, the distance between objects (whether large or small) subtly communicates the depth of their association. This 'proximity principal' can be used to aid our visual communications.

There are times when it can be beneficial, or even necessary, to present a close association or relationship with other objects, elements, people, places or things. As an example, in advertising, consider the highly prized, close association between a manufacturer of razor blades and a sports superstar. The value of this association runs to tens of millions of dollars. To benefit from the association, the sports star has to be presented in proximity to the item or brand.

Our Resources

Our Customers

Similarly, the greater the distance between items, the less the association.

Used intelligently, this 'proximity principal' can be applied to a visual aid to support a story, engineer a desirable conclusion or persuade an audience to agree with a specific point of view.

UP/DOWN AND LEFT/RIGHT

OK. So this is a somewhat simple point, but it still deserves to be understood, and used correctly to help you promote your message or messages.

We are born into a world of conventions. These are agreed and accepted standards or norms regarding what things are, or what things mean. These conventions are often unspoken – and can remain out of sight to most people.

It is a common convention to behave in a certain way when you step into an elevator. The rules, as such, have never been written down and you have never been trained in them. However, you will behave in a certain way, and you will expect others to behave in a similar way when riding an elevator. This is an example of an unspoken convention.

Now, in your mind's eye, imagine a map of the world – what do you see?

My guess is that you have a picture in your mind of a standard 'map of the world'. The one that was on the wall of your classroom at school, maybe. The one where Europe is situated in the middle, upper section of the map. The Americas are to the left and Russia and China to the right. Africa, South America and Australia dominate the lower half of the map. Right?

Is this a true depiction of the world? Well, not in all ways. However, this 'map' is the conventional one. The map that has been most used over time, although it may surprise you to know that it is not, in many ways, the most accurate one. This map (commonly known as the Mercator Projection map) is by far the best when it comes to navigation, but to achieve this, it also maintains a number of significant anomalies.

For instance, in the Mercator map, Alaska has a similar land mass to Brazil. Yet Brazil is nearly five times larger than Alaska. Finland is presented as having a similar north/south distance as India – yet, in reality, India's is much greater (by the way, the Mercator Projection was designed by a Norwegian).

Without straying too far from the point here, it is important to realize that we have underlying associations with regards to how things are presented. Top-down is a convention and is used to signify a hierarchy of sorts (be it significance, order of priority, alphabetic order). Even if your points are not numbered, convention will dictate that the item at the top of a list is seen as being more important or pertinent than the item at the bottom.

We can and should use top-down if it helps to support our communication and point of view. The same can also be said of 'left/right'.

For Westerners, the conventional direction for reading and writing is from left to right. If you were to create a slow-build visual communication that grew unconventionally from right to left, or from the bottom right-hand corner up to the top left-hand corner, you would have to have a good reason for doing so. Otherwise, it would probably cause confusion and undermine your point.

It is worth understanding conventions and applying them for effect, impact, understanding and persuasion.

1	2	3
4	5	6
7	8	9

✓

1	4	7
2	5	8
3	6	9

✓

9	1	8
7	2	5
3	6	4

✗

SCALE

When you claim that a drawing has been drawn to scale, your audience is led to believe that the proportions of the drawing are all correct – even though the drawing, which sits on a single sheet of A2 paper, represents a gigantic super-structure of some sort (maybe a suspension bridge, or a sky-scraper).

To help the viewer to appreciate the scale of something, it is common practice with maps and architectural drawings, to provide a reference such as: 1cm equals 10m or 1cm equals 500 miles. In photographs, it is common to place an object into the frame so the viewer can fully appreciate the size and scale of the subject matter by comparison.

As far back as the 17th century, it was common to use depictions of people in technical and architectural drawings to provide a natural scale reference for size and perspective.

The natural ability of an audience to accept, understand and appreciate scale provides us with many opportunities to communicate more clearly the point we wish to make.

The 20th Century

1900   1999

With reference to scale, we can present a horizontal line and claim it represents 100 years, or maybe 1,000 years or even 10,000,000 years. Your viewer will scale up and scale down accordingly.

2015

January   December

We can choose to present things in granular detail, thereby taking something that is, in actuality, very small and presenting it as very large. This is common in the comparison graphs that often accompany financial services advertisements. A bar chart representing the performance of three different funds can be presented in such a way that the difference between them will seem negligible, as it is undetectable. Yet, with a shift in scale, the same performance can be made to appear very significant indeed, with one of the performances seemingly 'head and shoulders' above the others. To be deemed 'head and shoulders' above something else would usually mean a significant difference in size – and yet with a simple shift in the scale used, a small difference can be made to look like a large difference. Similarly, an enlarged image of the mandibles of an ant can make it look like a fearsome creature, yet the same ant scurrying across the floor at your feet will just look like an ordinary insect. Thus, the scale of the things we represent can be used to persuade, influence and engage your audience.

STYLE

Many years ago, I was running a team-building workshop, and as part of an exercise on the importance of 'excellence', I wrote up a flip chart list of key 'talking points' that were offered up by the group. The list used bullet points, and although there was a top-down sequence, this was due to the order in which they were shouted out, and not due to an apparent order of importance.

After the workshop ended, I was approached by one of the participants who suggested that, although the topic (of excellence) was valid, she felt my style of handwriting and my group facilitation technique did not lend themselves to supporting the concept of excellence.

Clearly, for this person, 'excellence' had strong associations with neatness, order and structure – and my style of presentation undermined it for her.

I too make judgments about people, depending on how they look, how things are laid out, how things are organized and so on.

With this in mind, consideration must be given to the style of a visual communication. If you want to promote 'traditional values', the 'establishment', 'uprightness of character' or 'order' then a font such as Times New Roman or a similar grand font could be used.

If you want your communication to be infused with bohemian, anti-establishment sensibilities then borrowing the colours and style of an Andy Warhol print or the 1970's punk movement might help.

Think about the type of colours to be used.

Think about any font you will use.

Think about how everything will be organized. Will it convey structured thought, logic, artistic expression, excellence or mediocrity?

The Visual Communications Book

The Visual Communications Book

The Visual Communications Book

The Visual Communications Book

THE VISUAL COMMUNICATIONS BOOK

The Visual Communications Book

If a butterfly fluttering its wings above the Pacific ocean can have an impact on the ocean's waves and our global weather conditions, then know that the given style of your presentation can (and will) have an effect on your audience.

ORDER AND SEQUENCE

If I begin a sentence with the words "Once upon a time...", then you will understand what is about to follow. Yes, that's right...a fairy tale. Maybe you will not know exactly which fairy tale will follow, but you know it is likely to contain a cast of interesting characters (perhaps a prince and princess, a wicked witch, a wolf), some magic, a forest, some great threat to the existence or happiness of the main character – and a final resolution. You will also know that the story will officially end with the words: "...and they all lived happily ever after."

We have grown up (and our minds have developed) in a culture in which stories, poems, songs, sermons, speeches, TV programmes, movies and more have a 'beginning', a 'middle' and, of course, 'an end'.

Similarly, the order and sequence in which you present your ideas is important. Logic should determine the correct order. For example, in a business proposal, one type of logical sequence would be as follows:

- An introduction
- The issue, challenge of objective
- Review the 'as is' or current situation
- Consider the 'to be' or desired situation
- The proposed solution
- Why you have selected it as your recommendation
- What the solution is
- How it will be delivered
- Why this solution/proposal should be selected
- The investment needed and the likely financial return
- A summary of the objectives and valued benefits

This order of explanation has the benefit of being logical and understood by experienced business people. Reverse order wouldn't work, and it would not be as effective if two or three of the major slots were switched around. So, be sure to consider the logical order and sequence in terms of the narrative or story you wish to present.

Some of your needs may be served with a very simple three step process: A, then B, then C.

Others may require a more lengthy, detailed presentation: A, then B, then C, then D, then E, then F, then G, H, I, J and finally K.

REPRESENTING CONCEPTUAL GAPS

There are times when you are trying to bring others round to your point of view that you can use the power and potential of visual communications to drum up support for your cause. To do so, you will need to present your audience with an insight into a current issue, or a problem, a possible challenge, or (if in politics), an impending and inevitable crisis.

With this persuasion motive in mind, you could use visual methods to make the problem appear really small and insignificant or, alternatively, you could make the impending crisis look very dramatic and potentially life-threatening to all of humanity (I am thinking here of how global warming is often presented to the public). Without going to either of these extremes there are many opportunities to use visual methods to present a wide range of topics and potential gaps.

At its core, a 'gap' is the objective difference between two states. One state can be considered as the 'as is': the way it is now. The alternative state is the 'to be': the way it should, could or will be.

The gap between each of these states can be presented in a variety of ways: as contrasting graphs; as comparable bar charts; as data points set on a linear scale.

The key to promoting your chosen point is to select the scale used in your diagram so that you effectively frame and present your suggestion (or conclusion).

If your proposal recommends that your customer, or your company, invests £1m in your proposed project, then depending on how your customer or company would consider a £1m investment (it might be seen as very large, or very, very small depending on its own relative size) – you can scale your gap to be viewed as appropriate; anywhere from insignificant to earth-shattering.

These all represent the same gap. However, the larger gap looks a better fit for a large investment.

We can also use this method to make subjective gaps appear objective and measurable.

Consider a proposal to invest in a project to improve staff morale. By using a linear scale between one and 10 you can ask your audience members to give you a number to represent the current 'as is' measure. Having made the appropriate mark on the measure, you can now ask for a number to represent where they would like it to be. Having made that mark, you have visually, measurably and objectively represented the perceived gap. Used correctly, this is a very powerful tool for persuasion.

MOVEMENT

In art, the ability to portray movement requires great skill. Cartoonists are perhaps the best at capturing physical movement, and one only needs to look at a comic book to see how effective the cartoonists are with their use of body movement, air curves, visuals and word-based sound effects.

In our world of visual communications, we are less likely to need those fine artistic skills, although we may well, at times, be called upon to portray some form of movement or change in our illustration. For example, this could be a sequence of events presented in the form of stepping stones; a change in direction in a systems diagram; a state of progress or regression; a switching of positions, even.

In this world, the range of movement we need to present is more abstract. We present movement through varying steps or suggestions of steps.

In a two-dimensional illustration, lines, arrows and labels (in the form of numbers or letters) are useful tools that we can use to express movement and progression. Their effective use can help us to represent direction and order of sequence.

With three dimensions, and with greater artistic ability, you can also use perspective to convey movement as you literally have an extra dimension with which to work.

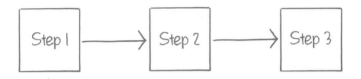

Clearly, when using some form of slide animation, the potential for illustrating movement is considerable. However, most people are unimpressed by this effect as it is usually cumbersome and often inappropriate. A first viewing of a Prezzo presentation (where the audience perspective constantly changes and moves in and out in a very fluid way), is likely to impress – however, with subsequent exposure to more and more presentations, you find that the novelty factor wears off pretty quickly.

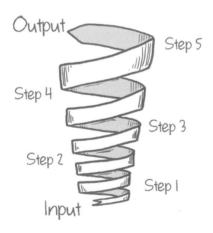

TIME

It is often useful, and sometimes even necessary, to incorporate the concept of time into a piece of visual communication. This can be done in a variety of ways, depending on what it is that you are trying to illustrate.

A typical basic, clock face is one method of presenting time. By adding arrows and changing the hand position you can suggest relatively modest (or even exaggerated) passages of time.

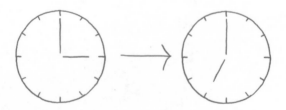

The famous 'evolution of man' image presents a timeline of many thousands of years in a series of five evolving images.

The passage of time can also be presented along a simple line. Generally, it makes sense for the line to be positioned horizontally and for time itself to be seen to travel from left to right: it just seems to be easier for people to understand it this way. The line can then be populated with events or signposts to illustrate progress or some other concept. In this way, it can be presented as part of a progressive journey and we are able to present time as something with quasi-physical characteristics.

SIMILARITY

As the mind derives meaning from the way that information is organized and presented, it also attributes relationship and association to items that are seen to look similar and vice versa. This similarity may relate to visual characteristics such as the colour, shape, size and position used. The greater the similarity, the greater the association. The smaller the similarity: the smaller the association.

To leverage the similarity principle, consider the various elements of information that you wish to present. Which elements would benefit from association with other elements? Can they be connected in some way by using the same colour, by enclosing them in the same shaped container, by making them the same size or by positioning them in proximity to one another (or maybe by applying all of them at the same time)?

To use a musical analogy, the similarity principle is about creating a visual harmony so that two or more objects create a single chord. Just as two, three or more notes, can harmonize to form a single, coherent musical chord.

By connecting various elements using the similarity principle, you can subtly develop a strong base of positive association. To do this, you will need to analyze your illustration and the various elements involved, and then determine the relationships and associations that will ultimately work for you and for your message.

SYMMETRY

Our world is full of visual symmetry, proportion and balance. Just picture Leonardo Da Vinci's Vitruvian Man, a butterfly, or even the Union Jack flag.

The human face has symmetry. The left- and right-hand sides of the face are equal, balanced and proportional; however, when you look in detail, you will find that the symmetry is rarely as perfect as it seems to be at first. One eye is perhaps slightly larger than the other, or seems to sit on a different horizontal line.

Imperfections aside, symmetry provides balance, harmony, proportion and beauty, and it is a useful aid in the way we present things visually.

Symmetry can be used as part of any visual or graphical illustration to frame part of your message. If you seek to present your information so that it is seen as being complete, then effective use of vertical or horizontal symmetry (or both) can help. The mind makes a natural association between various elements or forms that are presented in a symmetrical arrangement – and by using other graphical tools like proximity, colour and size you can further define any sub-groups that exist within the larger form.

Whatever the 'visual real estate' with which you are working, be it landscape, portrait, slide, sheet, whiteboard or whatever, think "centre, left and right, top and bottom".

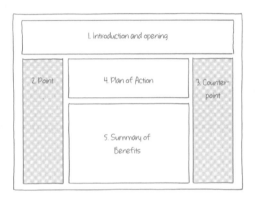

In situations where 'balance' is to be integrated into, or presented as part of, the message itself then using a bilateral symmetry to present both the point and the counterpoint is recommended. The architectural form of a doorway, with columns to the left and right, capped with a strong lintel or canopy is a perfect example of physical bilateral symmetry and conveys strength and stability. To leverage those same traits of strength, stability and balance, present your images or talking points in a bilateral way.

Conceptual opposites or counterpoints make more sense when presented on opposite sides; this placement goes to reinforce the oppositional relation of the points themselves. Think "positives and negatives; challenges and objectives; past and present; strategy and tactics". These are all terms for concepts which have a symmetrical, oppositional or dualistic nature.

COMPARE AND CONTRAST

There are times when you may wish to present two or more subjects for comparison. These could be ideas, propositions, specifications, competitors or two or more options of another kind. As part of a visual representation, your method of comparison and contrast should allow your audience to identify and appreciate areas of similarity, as well as identifying areas of slight or significant difference. You may then wish to focus attention on the similarity or difference for other purposes.

There are lots of methods for supplying data in a way which facilitates comparison and contrast. Graphs, tables and Venn diagrams are just a few of the options.

Anytime you put information side by side, you invite a comparison of sorts. Two upright rectangles, side by side, where one is 50% taller than the other, beg the viewer to compare them. Add some specific data to the illustration by placing a number in each (for example, £100m in the first, and £150m in the second) along with a title under each such as '2013 Revenues' and '2014 Revenues' – and the comparison is complete.

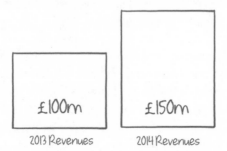

The message: strong past growth and likely future gains.

However, if the image is preceded by rectangles for £450m, £510m and £470m (for the years 2010, 2011 and 2012), then the illustration presents a very different message, suggestive of past glories and a very large drop in revenues.

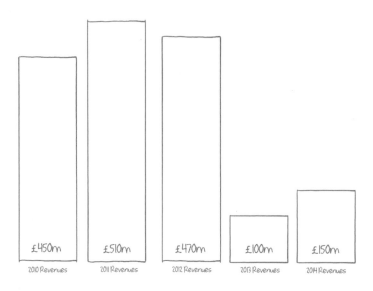

One method might work well to win new investors, whereas the other might serve as a vehicle for maintaining investor confidence. Sure, there was a collapse a few years ago, but it has been addressed and numbers are now heading north again.

The financial services industry is the master at presenting its performance (and that of the competition) in such a way. *Caveat emptor*.

INFORMATION DENSITY

Audiences automatically assume meaning from the way information is organized and presented to them. If the information is too sparse, the inference is that there isn't much important material; if it is too dense, an audience can easily become overwhelmed and anxious.

Think back to the hundreds or thousands of PowerPoint slides that have passed before your eyes. At one end of the information density spectrum there are slides which deliver very little content; maybe three of four bullet points with a word beside each point. Even though there may be plenty of information contained within the verbal commentary that accompanies the slide, the slide itself delivers extreme simplicity and is guilty of 'dumbing down' the topic.

At the other end of our spectrum there are the slides that are usually introduced by an embarrassed presenter saying something like, "There's a lot of information on this slide, and most of you won't be able to make out the detail on it. Sorry."

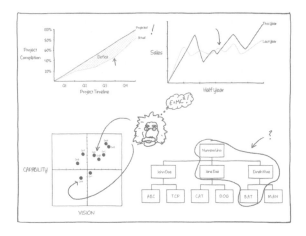

This presenter has used a crowbar to cram into their slide as much information as possible – and most audiences will assume that some of the information being presented is superfluous. A quick scan through the information being presented and their assumption will be confirmed.

Finding a happy medium to the information density challenge requires you to ask yourself a few questions – and to answer them truthfully.

1. What am I trying to communicate?
2. Is it absolutely necessary to my overall objective?
3. What information do I need to present to support this aim?
4. What is a 'must have'?
5. What is a 'nice to have'?

Your answers to these questions will tell you all that you really need to know. Create/re-work/update your communication and walk through the list once again to determine your final draft.

ENGAGING MINDS WITH BUILDS AND ANIMATION

One of the most incredible facts about the human brain is its role in forming our perception of things. The brain has acquired an incredible capacity for taking in chunks of visual data and 'filling in' the gaps in between them. This means that the brain can process 'more with less'.

This gap filling activity can also be seen in the way that your brain can also unscramble jumbled letters. Forget the Enigma machine, the human brain is the original code-breaker. Just look at the way your brain engages with the following information.

7HI5 M3554G3

53RV35 70 PROV3

HOW TH3 MIND C4N

3NGAG3 WI7H CON73N7

4ND DO 4M4ZING

7HINGS!

Did you even have to try and 'make it happen'? No. The brain just naturally seeks to fill in gaps, close loops, square circles and break codes, all so that you can complete your understanding.

Now, let's transpose this concept onto the world of visual communications. This potential for brain engagement is especially powerful when used as part of some kind of graphical build or animation. The build itself might be taking place on a sheet of paper, a whiteboard or even an animated slide as part of a presentation.

Until the white space or 'real estate' is seen to be complete, then your audience's cognitive powers will be working away as part of its natural tendency to close the loop and fill in the gaps. Their minds will always be endeavouring to solve the puzzle. In pursuit of completion, your audiences will seek additional insights or information to complete the picture. Information can be layered and delivered in different ways and in varying sequences, ensuring that your audience's sensory arousal, curiosity and interest are maintained alongside a nagging sense of uncertainty which will eventually lead them to their "Aha!" moment.

So, imagine your presentation of information as a puzzle of sorts, delivered and sequenced in part or in whole – and let your audience's minds engage and solve it.

SUMMARY AND CLOSE

As I stated at the beginning of this book, we really do live in a visual world, and by working your way through the preceding pages, you have demonstrated your own curiosity and interest in this subject.

I sincerely hope that what you have read has stimulated you and provided you with new ideas, insights and understanding. I really do believe that our ability to communicate can only be improved by the effective use of visual aids.

I predict that, in the years to come, you will begin to see more and more business books using visual communication. There are already quite a few on my own bookshelf.

Newspapers, magazines and websites are all becoming more graphical and more illustrative. Even software applications are now presenting complex data in simple, clean, infographic formats – to appeal to users and to meet their aesthetic expectations.

By incorporating a suite of visual tools, frameworks, models and principles into your own approach you will find that your ability to get your point across improves, and that, with time, you will develop a unique approach that works perfectly for you – and for your audience.

ABOUT THE AUTHOR

MARK EDWARDS has spent 20 years as an independent business consultant – creating visual abstractions, illustrations, models and diagrams to help some of the world's leading organizations to better communicate their insights, solutions, and propositions.

Contact the author for advice, training, or speaking opportunities:

mark.edwards@whiteboardstrategies.co.uk

years

building on our success

- 1993 Madrid
- 2007 Barcelona
- 2008 Mexico DF & Monterrey
- 2010 London
- 2011 New York & Buenos Aires
- 2012 Bogota
- 2014 Shanghai & San Francisco